AMAZING HUMAN FEATS OF Speed

by Debbie Vilardi

raintree
a Capstone company — publishers for children

Raintree is an imprint of Capstone Global Library Limited, a company incorporated in England and Wales having its registered office at 264 Banbury Road, Oxford, OX2 7DY – Registered company number: 6695582

www.raintree.co.uk
myorders@raintree.co.uk

Edited by Meg Gaertner
Designed by Becky Daum
Production by Craig Hinton
Originated by Capstone Global Library Ltd
Printed and bound in India

ISBN 978 1 4747 7517 5
22 21 20 19 18
10 9 8 7 6 5 4 3 2 1

ISBN 978 1 4747 7341 6
23 22 21 20 19
10 9 8 7 6 5 4 3 2 1

British Library Cataloguing in Publication Data
A full catalogue record for this book is available from the British Library.

Acknowledgements
We would like to thank the following for permission to reproduce photographs: AP Images: Hannibal Hanschke/picture-alliance/dpa, 16–17; Getty Images: John van Hasselt/Corbis Historical, 14–15, Walter Michot/Miami Herald/MCT/Tribune News Service, 7; NASA: JSC/NASA, 25, 26–27; Shutterstock: Africa Studio, 30–31, Chuck Wagner, 10–11, Dominik Michalek, 5, 28, Joshua Rainey Photography, 23, Maridav, 8–9, Melqianbao, 13, Rena Schild, 19, Roberto Caucino, cover, Yuri Turkov, 20–21. Design Elements: iStockphoto, Red Line Editorial, and Shutterstock Images.

Every effort has been made to contact copyright holders of material reproduced in this book. Any omissions will be rectified in subsequent printings if notice is given to the publisher.

CONTENTS

CHAPTER 1

SPEED

How fast is fast? The answer to this question varies. People race each other to see who is the fastest. Sometimes they walk or run. Sometimes they race with vehicles such as bikes and cars.

People have been racing since long ago. It takes hard work to be the fastest. It takes amazing feats of speed.

Athletes often run on special racing tracks.

CHAPTER 2

FAST Walker

Inês Henriques is a race walker from Portugal. She walks as fast as some people run. Henriques walked a 50-kilometre (31-mile) race in 2017. She set a world record. A few months later she broke that record.

She walked the same distance and cut two minutes from her time. Her new record was 4 hours, 5 minutes and 56 seconds. Her average pace was roughly 12.2 kilometres (7.6 miles) per hour. Now that's fast walking!

Race walkers must be in contact with the ground at all times.

CHAPTER 3

BLADE RUNNING

Sophie Kamlish is a para-athlete. Sophie was born with a medical problem. When she was nine years old her lower right leg had to be cut off. But this did not stop her becoming a **sprinter**! Kamlish runs with a special blade.

Kamlish's running blade is specially fitted to her leg.

RECORD BREAKER

Kamlish races in the 100-metre event. She raced in the 2016 **Paralympics** in Brazil. She broke the world record in a **heat**. Her time was 12.93 seconds. She came fourth in the final race.

But she beat her own record months later. It was at the 2017 World Para Athletics Championships. Her time was 12.9 seconds. Her speed made her a world champion.

Marchand cycled around an indoor track as he tried to beat his own record.

Many people came to support Marchand as he set a new record.

Marchand's 2017 speed was 22.5 kilometres (14 miles) per hour. But he was in a new age group. He set a record for those aged 105 and older.

Marchand proves that people of all ages can ride bikes. He stopped racing in early 2018. He was 106 years old.

SCENIC ROUTE

Marchand cycled 600 kilometres (370 miles) across Europe when he was 89 years old.

CHAPTER 5

RACING Legend

Some car races use large oval tracks. Drivers zoom around at high speeds. Other races have tight turns. Some races last a few hours. Others go on for a whole day. Juan Pablo Montoya has won all of these kinds of races.

Montoya has been racing since 1981.

A pit crew changes the tyres and adds fuel to the car in certain races.

Montoya began by driving **go-karts**. Now he drives racing cars. In 2005 he set a speed record in a **Formula 1 car**. He reached a speed of 372.6 kilometres (231.5 miles) per hour.

CHAPTER 6

ON THE Ball

Aroldis Chapman first played baseball in Cuba. Then he joined the Cincinnati Reds team in the United States. He threw the fastest **pitch** ever. The ball travelled at 169.1 kilometres (105.1 miles) per hour. Chapman later played for the Chicago Cubs. He repeated his fastest speed in 2016.

WORLD SERIES WIN

The Chicago Cubs won the World Series in 1908. Then they faced a long losing streak. It lasted more than 100 years. Aroldis Chapman helped them to win again in 2016.

Chapman now plays for the New York Yankees.

FREE-FALLING

Skydivers jump from aeroplanes. They use parachutes to land safely. Felix Baumgartner began skydiving at the age of 16. He took the sport to new heights in 2012.

A helium-filled balloon lifted a capsule into the sky. He dived from the capsule. He wore a spacesuit. This is because his dive began very high in the sky. It is very cold up there. The air is thin.

Skydivers enjoy free fall before they pull their parachutes.

Baumgartner jumped from this capsule when he set his record.

BREAKING RECORDS

Baumgartner jumped from 39 kilometres (24.2 miles) high. The jump lasted only 4 minutes and 20 seconds. His top speed was 1,357.6 kilometres (843.6 miles) per hour. It is the fastest dive on record.

WORLD RECORDS

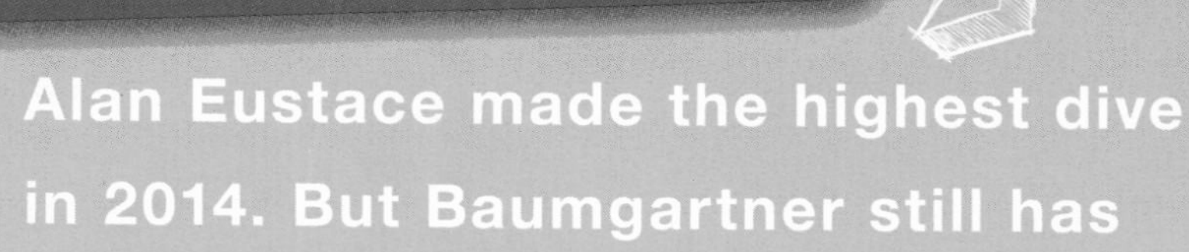

GLOSSARY

go-kart
small motor vehicle used specifically for racing

heat
race that determines which runners move on to the final

Formula 1 car
special racing car that holds one person and does not have a roof

Paralympics
major sporting competition in which athletes with disabilities compete

pitch
throw the ball to the hitter in baseball

sprinter
somone who runs as quickly as possible

OTHER AMAZING FEATS

- Usain Bolt became the fastest man alive in 2008. He broke the world record in the 100-metre sprint. His record is 9.58 seconds. He has won gold at this distance in three Olympic Games. He also holds gold medals in the 200-metre race.

- Jingli Duan has medals from the Rio Olympics and the World Rowing Championship. Her personal best time is for the 2,000-metre rowing event at 6 minutes and 41 seconds.

- Kadeena Cox is a Paralympic medallist in cycling and track. Cox has a medical condition. Her brain sometimes cannot control her muscles. She doesn't let this stop her, though. She set a world record in 2016 for the 500-metre cycling event. She did it in 37.5 seconds.

ACTIVITY

RACE THE CLOCK

Find out how fast you are! Use a stopwatch to measure seconds. Record the time as you complete one of these activities. You can also make up your own races.

- Run 100 metres.
- Skip around the park.
- Cycle to a friend's house.

FIND OUT MORE

Amazed by these record-breakers and curious about the science behind speed? Check out these resources:

Books

Car Science, Richard Hammond (DK Children, 2011)

Record Breakers!, DK (DK Children, 2018)

The World's Fastest Cars (World Record Breakers), Sean McCollum (Raintree, 2017)

The World's Greatest Olympians (The Olympics), Michael Hurley (Raintree, 2012)

Websites

Learn about how the Olympics first began.
www.bbc.com/bitesize/articles/z36j7ty

Find out more about speed.
www.dkfindout.com/uk/search/speed

INDEX